Praise for "What Still Matters"

Johanna Ely's book, *What Still Matters,* matters more than ever! It is a joy to read. The accessible 57 poems explore in strong, clear, yet evocative language, life's everyday themes from longing, nature, love, and dreams, to poetry itself.

—*Nina Serrano, Poet, Author, Film Maker, and Radio Host/ Producer*

Nature is the protagonist of Johanna Ely's new poetry collection, *What Still Matters*. Redolent with the sounds, colors, scents, and textures of the natural landscape, these poems are stitched with the yearnings and questions of the human heart. In lush, vibrant language, the poet leads us through an array of landscapes: wild gardens, the night sky, the desert, etc. There is gravitas, too, and stark imagery amid the beauty, as in these lines from the wildfire poem, "Fog:" *After the fires / it comes as an old grey dog / whose wet tongue licks / and cools the burned skin /*
of the earth. Readers will feel satiated by richness and precision of Ely's language and use of metaphor.

--*Sandra Anfang, author of Finishing School (2023) from Kelsay Books.*

What Still Matters

poems by
Johanna Ely

Copyright © 2023 by Johanna Ely

ISBN:979-8-9875209-3-2
Library of Congress Control Number: 2023912218

Cover Art:
Produced with Bing Image Creator, using the prompt
"Irises as seen in a dream"

Edited by Mary Eichbauer

Cover Design by Deborah L. Fruchey

Last Laugh Productions, 2023
125 Conifer Lane
Walnut Creek, CA 94598
lastlaughproductions.org

What Still

Matters

each, yes,
each moment
is its own cathedral—
the pillars, arched ceilings,
the stained glass

light comes in
from somewhere else

one enters, wanders
dumbstruck,
until moved along
by a gentle but inexorable
hand
into the next one

—*Diane Lee Moomey*

Table of Contents

Part III: A Flock of Magpies

Part IV: Tossing the Sticks

Foreword

"I am what remains."
　　　—Johanna Ely

Johanna Ely's poetic voice bears witness to the world—our broken world, that gorgeous, overblown rose—in all its loveliness and imperfection. These poems carry the voice of a devoted dreamer who transforms endings into radiant beginnings, who records the wonders of the earth, even as she fears for their destruction. The poet fears for this fragile world, her hands filled with the broken things that make up a life. Through her eyes, we see beginnings and endings, set to the bittersweet music of the natural world.

The poet's mind is not stagnant—it is transformational. She divines the secrets of nature from what is around her—the sounds and scents of life, the dance of trees in the wind. She gives nature its voice, conjuring life out of fragile things, found things. A tiny seashell unearthed on an arid path plunges us into the ocean. A simple feather, found on the grass, waits for her to find more feathers, enough to make the poet a pair of wings. The poet wanders, seeking her muse, who appears in mundane guise—a tangible muse for a dreamer whose feet are rooted in the real.

These poems are embedded in place and time, in the present of here-and-now and in memory. Moments when hope flags in the face of tragedy, when the poet witnesses fire and extinction, she resorts to dreams, where mythical figures dwell in the stars, sailing down the Milky Way. Love never dies, though people do. Cycles evoke the goddess, giver of life, who nurtures the stories we tell to keep ourselves alive.

Johanna Ely knows the transformative powers of the imagination, of dreams, of a life in nature. As natural as flowers, these poems bud and bloom, exploding into blossoms ripe as flesh, as sweet and present as memories of youth and love.

"This breath of wonder / never the last breath."

Mary Eichbauer
A Poet for our Fragile World

I Want the Word

I want the word

tender
to be the first word in a poem.
I want a poem about tenderness.

Tender rose petals, easily torn.
Tender wound, not yet healed.
Tender song, still unsung.

Give the world tenderness—
stroke hair,
gently wipe away tears.
Soon, a sparrow will build a nest
in your arms,
a pine tree will teach you its language,
a swallowtail will flutter in your hair.

Have tender regard for the moon—
how she seems to gaze down tenderly
at your small, fragile body,
sending you her light.

Why I Keep Broken Things

I treasure what's broken,
what isn't whole—
pieces of seashell,
a cracked ceramic cup,
a silver necklace missing a clasp,
a book with torn pages.

I keep the single turquoise earring,
the black sock that no longer has a mate.

Sometimes, I think I should put
what's been damaged
or has a missing part
in a large cardboard box—
say a prayer, light a candle,
then gently place the box in the trash.

But no, I want to save these
scraps of my imperfect life—
fragments of abalone shell from Mendocino,
a chipped teacup from Kyoto, beautifully glazed,
the tarnished necklace, a gift from a lover

who died years ago.

Sometimes, a single sock finds a new mate,
two mismatched earrings make a lovely pair.

How wonderful to keep
the tattered book,
its last two pages missing—
knowing that whoever reads it
will make up a new ending.

Letter to Frida Kahlo

Dear Frida,

You stare at me willfully
from the cover of a magazine,
your eyebrows a bridge
over two dark moons.
I try to read your unblinking eyes,
the words behind your closed red lips.

You wear gold earrings
laden with pearls,
a twisted gold necklace
wrapped around your throat.
Your hidden scars are clothed in bright colors,
your blouse the deep blue of a tropical sea.
Vines of hot pink blossoms
embroidered on neck and shoulders,
a purple ribbon braided into your thick, black hair,
swept up with a crown of marigolds.

I remember my pilgrimage
to your Casa de Azul—

the bus ride, the blocks
of walking towards you.
The house painters let us
take a look inside—
all your precious artifacts
stored on shelves.
I imagined you and Diego
sitting in the garden,
how he picked magenta roses for your hair.

Tell me why you loved him—
did the old bullfrog
croak out the names of stars?
Did you try to love yourself—
your body cracked open like a crab shell,
the wounded flesh almost
too tender to touch?

Your self-portraits
honored broken things—
the dead hummingbird
that hung around your neck
from a necklace of thorns
and snapped twigs.

Yet, you of broken body and heart,
refused to stay broken.

You stare at me willfully.
I think your dark eyes say:
Be brave. Paint the sorrow.
Find your own path to the sea.

The Circus

Every summer in late August,
I pretend the circus comes to town.
I want to run away with a dark-eyed acrobat,
be the beautiful woman who enters the ring
sitting regally on the back of a towering elephant,
share my saddest secrets with a clown.

At 4am I hear the trucks roll in,
heading towards First Street.
Instead of circus folk,
vendors set up small white tents
selling "treasures" from the past—
old furniture, dresser drawers overflowing
with costume jewelry,
tables crowded with stuff I don't want—
painted beer mugs,
Hawaiian shirts and tie-dyed skirts,
empty Coca Cola bottles and tin signs.

I know
the wild animals
and acrobats will never

come here.

The aging elephant has been set free—

the man who swallows swords

remains a childhood fantasy.

Still, every year

I wake and listen

as trucks rumble by

in the pre-dawn darkness,

imagining the dangerous glint

in a tiger's eye—

dreaming how I could join the troupe

and disappear,

learn to walk the tightrope

without a net.

Morning Walk in Lithia Park

I wander into this landscape,
a creek running through me—
garble of water tumbling
over shadowy rocks
dappled with sunlight,
collage of leaves floating
in mirrors of blue sky.

This summer morning
aches to be discovered.
I walk past two young men
drumming to the sun god—
ducks float silently in a pond
rippling with azure and gold.

In the parking lot,
a pink and purple school bus
grins at me,
dolls' heads and dinosaurs
glued on the dash,
strings of lilac beads
hanging in the doorway.

For a few seconds
I crave the rambling life—
want to climb on board
without a map,
forget my way home.

Leaving Mendocino

Thirty years
I've been coming here
to hide in your morning fog,
banter with your ghosts—
long enough to remember the past
the way I want to remember it,
certain memories drowning
in the icy undertow
of lapis lazuli waves.

Some things don't change—
the hard crash of whitecaps
against sharp rocks,
a reminder that there are no
gentle beginnings or endings.

Each year, the stairs
are harder to climb,
the view from this
upstairs room still sublime,
the same church steeple
poking sky,

books and notebooks
piled on a low table,
my aching need
to write in solitude and silence.

Rhododendrons bloom,
pink and purple blossoms
tangled in dark branches.
Fallen red petals
stain a shady path,
the pungent smells
of pine and ocean
clean my heart,
the glass house on the cliff
smaller than I remember.
Fog returns at three.
Sunny wildflowers,
bell-shaped cups of gold,
wave goodbye.

This morning I realize
there may not be
a next time—
the light is different,

less familiar,
the faces on the street
are young, and I am not.

The restaurant
I used to go to
has closed,
no more Eggs Benedict
served on china plates
in a yellow garden room,
glass doors opening
to the sea—
scattered on the table tops,
brittle dried-up leaves.

Night Driving

I no longer see details.
The white lines on the road fade,
the turn-off signs blur,
the oncoming headlights
blind me.

Other drivers race by
in their sleek cars—
curse my hesitation,
my old woman ways.

They don't know that once
I loved speed
and driving all night,

when the boundaries
disappeared
and a hand on the thigh
in the dark

was a green light
to love,

on a journey
I never
wanted to end.

Questions

In the middle of the night,
in the dark cocoon of her room,
a place of silken dreams
and transformation,
she writes down
every question she has
about life and death.

Tapping her pen on the paper
reminds her of dripping rain,
the aftermath of a storm.
Her heart is tired of crazy weather,
fires burning in every season,
tears flooding the streets.

How peacefully her cat sleeps,
curled into a question mark,
while the answers she seeks
float around the room—
wise old souls,
invisible and silent.

On Sundays

I curl back into myself—
a snail retracting into
her whorled shell,
a water lily closing up
her pale pink petals
for the night.

On Sundays
I stay in my room
with the door shut—
eat poems instead of food,
dream of writing words on walls
in places I've never been.

On Sundays
I like to disappear—
even if I turned into dust,
there wouldn't be enough sunlight
in this cool, dark house
to illuminate my presence.

I'm the shadow within the shadow,
dancing happily alone.

The Ballet Studio

Next door to my house,
the ballet studio has
an outdoor stage
protected by a white tent.
At night, the tent breathes
in the wind,
rustles and flaps
like a restless swan
dancing in the darkness.

During the day,
notes of classical music
and old showtunes waft in
through my bedroom windows.
I hear the teacher snap her fingers,
count the beats.
I hear the thumps from landed leaps,
imagine young girls in black leotards
doing a plié,
bending at the knees,
lifting arms above heads,
fledglings learning to spread

their wings,
to land on a branch gracefully.
A yearning rises up in me,
a longing for another time
when all that mattered
was the dance.

On Saturday mornings
I hear the teacher tell
the five-year-old dancers
to pretend they are flinging
flower petals in the air.
It is autumn
and the roses are in decline,
but for the little ones
it's still spring,
and they are blossoming ballerinas.
How they must love to bend down
and gather the invisible pink petals
in their small rounded arms.

I stand in my bedroom,
scoop up wilted memories
with my wrinkled hands,

toss them clumsily
towards the ceiling,
not caring where they land.

When the teacher plays
Twinkle, twinkle, little star,
my eyes tear up.
I wish I was one of them,
a little girl
who still believes
that when the music starts
and the dancers twirl,
everyone twinkles and shines.

Cootie Catcher as Origami Flower as Poem-Maker

I am terrible at origami,
can't follow the steps,
complete the intricate folds—
wanting so badly
to make a box or a crane
out of delicate paper.

A poet reinvents a childhood game—
her cootie catcher
now a poem-maker.
I tell myself I can do this—
cut out the paper square,
print words inside
the smaller squares and triangles,
find an online video to remind me
how to fold the corners
into an origami flower
that opens and closes,
the way my heart
opens and closes,
filled with its old desires.

I remember when cooties
were the germs that girls and boys
could catch from touching each other—
how quickly we realized
we wanted that touch.

Cootie catcher,
fortune teller.
I pick one of four colors,
my fingers inside the flower,
its paper petals
opening and closing
as I spell *lilac,*
then the next word
and the next—
choosing each one carefully,
unfolding the hidden phrase,
finding my heart's poem:

lilac shadow
dream I emerge from
changed

Still Life of an Apple

I cut an apple in half—
its halves sit
balanced and still
on the cutting board,
two pairs of ears
listening.

Two seeds peek out
from fleshy, white halves.
Shadows render
two dark circles,
the eclipse of two moons.

I am as still and silent
as an apple,
cut open and exposed—
my eyes the color
of two small seeds
planted before summer ends,
my ears listening
to the whisper
of unborn trees.

Dancing with the Trees

On This First Day of January

I rejoice at rivulets of rain water,
at the return of the sun—
how it casts a glistening path
across the strait, silver light
touching velvety hills, silky blue sky.

I adore newborn grass,
logs and river rocks tinted
electric green,
tree trunks and branches
twisted into mossy sculptures.

I applaud fields of brown thistles,
a wiry yellow tree with no leaves,
wild orange daisies—
a rickety-rackety wooden fence
casting rickety-rackety shadows.

I celebrate puddles of shining light
on a muddy trail,
egrets hunting in low-tide muck,
the moon balanced on the fingertip
of a new year.

The Calligraphy of Winter

So quiet, this moment,
as if a Chinese master
had painted the calligraphy of winter
on soft, grey paper.
Rising up from morning mist,
tips of branches brushed in black ink,
and there, two snowy egrets sit,
perfectly balanced.
Between them, a tangled branch
takes the shape of a mountain,
a sign of strength, serenity.
Below them, calm water
reflects their silent beauty,
the harmony of light and shadow.
In this breath of stillness,
the edges of the world disappear,
sky and water become one,
and I, too, become still.

What to Be

Be rain.
Kiss a wildflower's lilac petals,
linger on a moth's eyelash,
moisten a lizard's sticky tongue.
Chase a slippery grasshopper
across a morning meadow
in the green of early spring.

Don't mourn
the end of the world—
what could've been,
what never was.

Be rain.
Tap gently on broken glass.
Be the sound of begin.

At the End of a Rainy Day

Goodbye
to a dark grey sky
with its slippery open wounds.

So long
to a sunset
whose slash
of raw pink flesh
heals into
a long white scar
just before
the light disappears.

Fog

After the fires,
it comes as an old grey dog
whose wet tongue licks
and cools the burned skin
of the earth.

This morning,
it comes as a gentle spirit
who glides through the meadow,
who wraps the charred trees
in soft grey gauze
as branches slowly green again.

Its thick silence
embraces us,
its mist of healing
falls upon us,
as we gladly walk
into its nebulous glow,
and, for a moment,
disappear.

Talking to the Roses

This year,
the old roses bloom early,
coaxed open
by a syrupy sun.

I watch them ripen,
grow plump and full—
petals unfolding
hidden shades of pink.

Huge roses,
heads as large
as an open palm—
my hands want to cup each face,
gently touch silky lips.

I won't cut them,
arrange them in a vase
to droop, to gasp
for light—

no, they will burst open,
explode under sun and sky

as breezes kiss
each falling petal.

Every morning
I will talk to them,
tell them they are beautiful.
The secrets we share,
no one will ever know.

A Song from Side B

On this spring afternoon,
the trail pulses with life—
dazzling orange poppies,
lacy anise,
the thrum of monarch wings.

Hungry bees buzz
in a sea of purple vetch.
Across the valley,
hills the color of gold pyramids.
Clouds line up in rows,
eager to hear a song.

Down in the eucalyptus grove,
sunlight shimmers
in leafy branches.
Long ribbons of bark
hang from the tall trees—
enough smooth wood
to build a boat.
Always,
the rustle of water.

Murmurs from a hidden stream
drift through yellow mustard blossoms,
the old fence line creaks
a melody—
noisy birds
join the chorus
of humming trees.
When the light turns amber,
the wind picks up—
strips of bark twist and flap
in the evening breeze.
Ghosts play percussion,
we sing the words.

What the Bee Discovers

Buzzing in the branches
of a cherry tree,
a bee discovers a galaxy
of a hundred round blossoms,
clusters of blushing stars
orbiting above the tree trunk
where the bee circles too,
then makes a soft landing
deep into the center of a
luscious pink planet,
eagerly exploring
its velvety inner terrain,
rear legs covered with galaxy dust,
a tiny astronaut traveling
from one bursting blossom
to the next,
lost in a nebula
of intoxicating scent.

California in Early May

I am drought.
My lakes are ancient mouths
filled with cracked mud.
My rivers are parched throats.

My hills are tinderbox brown,
my days too hot and brittle
for late spring.

I am the horrible
premonition of flames—
the memory of air
rancid with death,
sky blood orange.

My skin is dry,
paper-thin.
Put a match to me
and I will burn and scream—

explode with a blinding flash of light,
devour every dream.

Dancing with the Trees

What if one day
the trees in town
uprooted themselves—
miraculously moved towards the river
in a spectacular procession,
finally free to search for water
after years of drought.

What a sight that would be,
their long, thick roots gliding
down sidewalks, each tree
leaving behind a trail of falling leaves,
graceful branches swaying
their Buddha arms in the air,
long trunks creaking and groaning
after being tethered to the ground since birth.

As the trees pulled their roots out of the ground,
people would be frightened, feeling the earth shake.
Everyone would call to them, beg them to return,
stumble into the gaping holes they'd left behind.

I would follow the Japanese maple
out of the garden,
place my feet on its wizened roots,
wrap my arms around its trunk—
let it slow-dance me to the river,
the wind whistling an old love song.

Family of Trees

It is the trees who tell me I am loved.

The salty mangrove,
its long roots winding
around me like a river—
my secret stories protected
in its underwater arms.

The Japanese maple,
every autumn—
its red leaves flaming towards me,
unashamed.

The chestnut,
giving me its dark brown nut,
so smooth to touch—
a worry stone I rub with my thumb.

The pine tree,
the full moon singing in its branches—
a song I remember
from childhood.

Trees are the family I never had.
Their branches reach out,
embracing my silence.
Each leaf, an ear listening
to what I could never say.

The Shell

It is mid-July,
and I'm walking on a trail
that's as dry and cracked
as an old man's hands.
Yet, blue sky shimmers
above me,
as if I am underwater
looking up—
the clouds, long wavy
wisps of breath.

All around me is
the voice of water.
In the eucalyptus trees
I hear the whisper
of a creek,
while on the hill,
orange butterflies
are little fish who laugh
and flutter downstream.

I am protected

in the womb of the afternoon
as I swim through stalks of anise,
those bright underwater suns—
or admire artichoke flowers,
the spikey purple fish who drift
through ochre sea grass.

Looking down,
I find a white shell,
a tiny boat filled with
dirt instead of sand.
I wonder if it remembers
the smell of salt,
or tumbling in an ocean
millions of years old.
I pick it up, as if it is a promise
that someday water will return
to cover this land again,
and I, who believe in cycles,
dream of a boat
in the shape of a shell,
floating in a sea of stars.

Artichokes

I always think of them
as a rare delicacy,
though their ancestors
grow wild in California hills,
flowering brilliant purple in early summer.

How exotic to eat a thorny thistle
with my fingers,
to open a large bursting bud,
carefully pulling back
the steamy green bracts,
dipping each one in melted butter,
my teeth scraping off
the soft skin from each petal,
until only fuzzy choke
and heart remain.

Ah, the unprotected heart!
Supposedly the best part—
I leave it on my plate.
Perhaps you will crave
its fleshy sweetness,
so tender and exposed.

A Sky the Color of Oceans

The morning sky is a silent stone—
smooth, dense, ashy gray.
August's fires harden the hazy light,
as the sun, a blood-red garnet,
smolders above me.
Smoke from charred
trees, bones, and buildings
stings my teary eyes,
the metamorphic mix
of burnt plastic and molten metal
sears my lungs.

I'm a child who has grown old
and keeps asking what's gone wrong—
remembering those summers
when the sky was the color of oceans,
puffy clouds rolling across turquoise water,
gulls swooping down to touch lapis waves,
the light bright, the air fresh.
How when I looked up, I always thought
it would stay that aqua blue forever.

Hydrangeas in Late August

The hydrangea flowers,
once deep pink
and blue in spring,
find themselves at summer's end
fading into muted shades—
their petals thinned to brittle skin,
tinged with brown and gray.

A woman
cuts the long, stiff stalks,
carefully arranging the dried flowers
in a Chinese vase.

I am both the flowers
and the woman.
I am what remains.

September

The days turn towards each other,
then sigh and look away.

Summer is flying off with the geese
into a milky blue sky.

We want to believe
time will spiral
into endless lifetimes—

Eternity a circle we follow
around mountains trembling with joy,
lakes rippling with infinite stars.

A sun and moon
who wrap seasons
and tides around us—

Our hands filled
with dried tansy
and nautilus shells.

Mandalas of gold light
everywhere we look.

This breath of wonder
never the last breath.

Dreaming of Bamboo

1.

Sunlight through bamboo—
tall shoots sweep over me,
a wave of light and shadow.

2.

Water through bamboo leaves—
a glimmer of blue sparkle
seen through a fan of green.

3.

Peeking through a bamboo screen,
hidden from that other world.
Dry leaves speak their own language.
Further out, a train's whistle.

4.

This moment painted
through a bamboo window—
brush strokes of russet reeds,
silver sky, purple hills.
A white moth floats above yellow flowers,
small petal dancing.

5.

Sunlight through bamboo—
a dream I dreamed one autumn afternoon.

Ode to Golden Light

all afternoon
the light envelops me
in its magnificent aura
whispers to me
to return home and write a poem
in my mustard yellow house
assures me that the stucco walls
reflect the color of desert sand
ever shifting   changing
as the light grows larger
turning deeper gold
as the day becomes smaller
and everything glows brighter
than autumn's tawny leaves
the sun's spindly fingers
spun into shining threads
connecting tree to leaf   bird to sky
while I look through a camera lens
tinted the color of honeyed dreams
asking blindly   who holds
this wondrous camera to my eye

Clouds

How effortlessly the clouds change—
no promises to stay the same.

A silver goose,
wispy cirrus wings touching sky,
neck and legs stretched
long and lean by a strong wind,

chases a fork-tailed swallow
whose soft cumulus body glides
on breaths of air, its pointed beak
beginning to fade.

Both birds fly east
towards thin streaks of slate—
an illusion of misty mountain peaks
rising above the real mountain below.

Only for a moment
do clouds become the ancient dreams
we vaguely remember—
torn pieces of pearlescent silk

embroidered with turquoise threads of light.

Soon the birds have disappeared—
a thick blanket of grey
slowly covers the hazy blue.

How effortlessly the clouds change—
perhaps tomorrow, first rain.

October

It leaves a bitter aftertaste
though the season is sweet—
the way the light runs out
before we are through with the day,
the burning heat from a waning sun
that still presses against the skin,
a ragged sense of betrayal
by a month whose beauty astounds us,
just before the darkness slips in.

Bird of Paradise

Crane flower—
orange sunsets flare
in your crested crown.
You are November's queen.
As autumn days collapse
and burn,
your indigo tongue
sings of sky.

Which paradise do you rule?
A tropical place
humid with desire?
From your jungle-green sheath,
a strong, exotic bird emerges—
a geometric beauty
painted with a Cubist's brush.

Your pointed beak
sets direction—
as if you could grow wings
and fly beyond the confines of a vase,
to the limits of our dreams.

For the Winter Solstice

Winter paints this shortest day
the color of silence.
Among the dark roots of naked trees,
blood red leaves turn to mulch,
the blind worm seeks redemption.
A grey memory settles on the frozen land
of lost sun, waning moon.

On this longest night
there is a turning—
a pink rose shivers,
blooming defiantly in the cold wind.
Abandoned nests sleep in bare trees,
dreaming that spring returns as a bird.

Tonight,
flames will dance,
lovers will kiss.
The dead will come
and whisper in our ears,
their mouths filled with light.

A Flock of Magpies

A Flock of Magpies

for Weaving Girl

When you looked at him
across the Milky Way
it was love at first sight,
no turning back.

In that moment,
you stopped weaving
your father's shirts
with threads of silver light,
and your beloved
no longer herded stars
across vast skies
of ancient constellations.

You wanted the boy
whose eyes were amber moons,
made love with him
in soft grasses, light years away—
forgot the passing of time,
the unfinished shirts
that no longer shone,

the stars, who like dull cows,
wandered off into fields of galaxy dust.

Meeting each other only once a year
was the punishment you suffered
for your passionate spark.

Seventh month, seventh day—
in the midnight darkness
you burn with longing,
while a flock of magpies
forms a bridge of wings
over a river of stars.

Conjunctions

1.

On the longest night of the year
I searched the sky
for Jupiter and Saturn—
two planets
not on a path to collide,
simply coming so close
they seemed to shimmer
as a single, brilliant star—
the ancient promise
of returning light.

2.

I remember, years ago,
passing an old lover on the street,
a strange lingering light between us—
how we almost touched, but didn't,
my desire to feel the warmth of his embrace
the conjunction of memory and longing.

The Clean-Swept Heart

To sweep the heart clean
is not my desire.
My birch broom,
made of twigs and leaves,
sweeps away
fear and jealousy,
but not love,
not love.

My heart chambers
beat, pulse,
while I sweep away the dust
that settles on old friends.
Let me feel them stir
as the heart heaves
one more sigh.

As I sweep away the cobwebs
the dead leave behind,
let me hear their voices sing in my blood,
my fingers sticky
with silky strands of memory,
my heart thumping their names.

A Poet Revises *Luncheon on the Grass*
(a painting by Claude Monet)

Monet, imagine a more intimate, modern scene—
the admiring friends gone,
just a man and a woman sitting together
at a picnic table,
the ground too wet for a luncheon on the grass.
No elaborate cake or roasted chicken
offered up on a white tablecloth.
Instead, paint simpler pleasures—
the man cutting slices of avocado
and tomato with his pocket knife,
the woman spreading thick globs
of cream cheese on each slice.
Two cups made from a plastic water bottle
cut in half, the wine glowing a pale yellow.
Too early for summer peaches—
let them eat strawberries
that taste like forbidden kisses.
Let them lick cream cheese off their fingers.
Let them slowly realize they have fallen in love.
Paint them singing a song as they try to coax
the sun to peek out through gathering clouds.
In the almost deserted park,
add a man walking his dog

over the Japanese-style footbridge

reminiscent of Giverny,

or a woman following her child around the small pond

where grey sky reflects silver off black water

and your violet lilies float among moss-green leaves.

Emblazon with red the blackbird

who hops on the table,

your quick brushstrokes flitting across

the canvas like his wings,

while the man and the woman sit there

as long as the green jumble of light remains,

loving the same light you have always loved.

Waiting for My Muse

I sit on a bench at the water's edge,
waiting for you to walk by.
On this cold winter morning,
I imagine you wearing a black parka
and a green wool beanie
you pull down over your ears.

The egret knows who you are—
your missing shadow
hides in its snowy feathers.
I confess my desire to see you
to the marsh grasses—
they sway back and forth
in the sharp breeze,
hearing your silent voice.

I wait patiently all afternoon—
search the grey clouds
for your silver-blue eyes,
listen to the lonely cries

of wild geese winging overhead.

At twilight, before I walk home,
an owl swoops down from the broken sky,
a hint of your smile on its moon face.

Tonight, I will dream of you again.
You will come to me as I sleep
and whisper that one true line,
the one I will never remember.

Field Guides

I study the identification guide
for common wildflowers,
but the drawings are too small,
and only the California poppy
looks familiar.
It's the same with the guide for butterflies,
and the one for trees—
though I can recognize a live oak
by its dense green crown and spiky leaves.

I would like to be able to name them all,
point to a cluster of magenta flowers and shout,
I adore you, shooting stars!
or gently stroke a furrowed trunk
and whisper, *Hello, California laurel!*

The butterflies flutter and play,
tease me with their non-stop dance,
one moment so close,
then on to another branch,
another blossom.
Most are monarchs

or cabbage whites,
according to color and size,
but the one with gold eyes
on its chestnut brown wing
I call, *my love*—
believing your spirit is here,
flitting around this tall slender tree,
the one I can't identify.

Whale-of-a-Heart

I see a photo
of a blue whale's heart,
perfectly preserved—
an astounding sculpture
of arteries and muscle.

I learn that,
at four-hundred pounds,
it is the heaviest heart
on the planet—
that its aorta is the width
of a dinner plate.

I read that it is the size
of a golf cart,
the length of a couch.
Some people claim
that a small child
could swim through
its arteries
like a little fish.

I study this huge heart,
how it resembles
a hollow shell,
each empty passage
a mysterious tunnel to explore.

I think of you
and your whale-of-a-heart,
large enough to take me in,
how you let me live
in its beating chambers,
call it home—
your heart pumping life
back into the body,
both yours, and mine.

Birthday Poem for My Son

Born five days into the new year,
you will always be the one
who greets the light—
the winter sun flashing through you
cold and dazzling,
your strong bones holding you up
as you walk towards spring.

Your sign is Capricorn,
the goat with the fish tail,
lover of earth and water.
I watch you climb a mountain,
determined to reach its craggy peak—
then swim beneath the sea,
remembering your salty birth.

You are an old soul,
serious and persistent.
I have learned from you
how to see the winter trees differently—
how within their bare branches
the moon sits and grows larger
until everything shines.

Rainbows for Thelma

In her quirky feline way,
Thelma was obsessed with rainbows—
chased their wild, fiery dance
across the kitchen floor.

Crystals dangled on a string for her,
in a window above the sink—
a pendulum of prisms
swept back and forth,
flash of jewels
exploding on white cupboard doors,
brown linoleum floor.

Tiny iridescent dancers,
flitting here, there, everywhere.

She'd pounce on one,
another and another,
always a second too late,
mesmerized, hypnotized by dazzle,
not knowing which way to jump, to turn,
a frenzied ball of electric fur

determined to capture light
in all its blinding colors.

No longer a cat,
she's sunshine streaming
through a kitchen window
at three in the afternoon.

Crystals swing across glass,
catching its sparkle.
I still call her to come play—
rainbows whirling 'round me
in this room of glimmering stars.

Light, Hope, and Love

Praise the light that comes early
after the stars go out—
before the first bird wakes
and sings its joy to the setting moon.

Praise the glimmer of hope
we dream before dawn,
when night casts its shadow
along buildings and empty streets—
in dark rooms
where loneliness embraces
those who cannot sleep.

Praise love.
It is the song that stays late,
the candle that burns
after the light is gone.

Tossing the Sticks

Time of Poetry

In the beginning,
when cloud people walked
across a sienna clay sky,
Kokopelli spun his poems
on the desert mesas.
In his sack, he carried creation stories,
corn seeds, and unborn babies
longing for a mother's kiss.
His flute announced flying saucers
and red rock sunsets.
Twisting and turning
down indigo canyons,
he could change himself
into a clever snake,
a spiral of stars,
a circular dream spinning
on a sapphire river.
The owl,
the hawk,
and the eagle
dropped feathers in his honor.
The earth,

the sky,
and the water
sang his rain songs.
It was a time
of joy and enlightenment
for all who listened.
At twilight,
the sound of his flute
still drifts down the winding riverbed—
poems crooned by a trickster wind—
the faint outline
of a hump-backed shaman
dancing on canyon walls.

Poem

When dreams no longer mattered,
when I became too broken to write—
I walked to the marina,
listened to the clang of masts,
the silence of a cloudless sky.

I stood for a long time
looking at boats,
then noticed a plain one,
all white, moored
at the visitor's dock,
the word *Poem*
painted in ocean blue
on its stern.

I had almost given up
on taking such a journey,
but there she was,
this small sturdy boat
with a perfect name—
destination uncharted,
waiting for me to board.

Dreaming in the Time of the Pandemic

In my dreams
I've stopped searching
for a refuge to protect me
from death,
stopped trying to find
an abandoned house
laced with memories of wisteria
or a dark cave illuminated by candlelight,
my silent poems written only
for the petroglyphs.

Now I dream
with my eyes wide open—
memorize the shape of every tree,
the scent of roses bursting open
in the heat of spring,
the way the sunlight
warms my body
as I sit alone, facing west.

In my dreams,
we hold up our hands

and mirror each other,
place palms and fingers together—
promise we'll never stop touching.

The Rainbow

for Sargamo

She sleeps in a grey room,
her face turned away from voyeurs—
red high heels tossed on the floor
after a night of dancing.
The white sheet slips
from her naked hips,
long ebony hair cascading
over the edge of the mattress
the way water tumbles over a cliff,
filling a pool with darkness.

One guardian sits in an armchair,
the other stands
at the foot of her bed.
If she saw them,
she would call them angels,
even though they don't have wings.

Her tiny dog perches on the headboard,
faithfully guarding his mistress
as she dreams a magnificent rainbow—

purple hyacinth and scarlet maple,
iridescent hummingbird and russet fox,
ochre mountain and azure ocean,
brushed across the room in a sweeping arc.

Even Death,
disguised as an old lover,
peeks out from under her bed
and looks up in amazement,
forgetting to whisper her name.

Feathers

I found a feather in the driveway—
small, gray, ragged, ordinary.
It didn't matter
that I couldn't name the bird
who had dropped it—
it was a gift.

I picked it up,
studied it—
smoothed its edges
into a soft, tapered leaf.

Each feather I find,
an extraordinary treasure.

I collect them,
different colors and sizes,
hang them from the bedroom ceiling.
Soon, I will make a pair of wings.

A Poet's Dream

I dream I am an artist,
showing my work on the floor
of an empty house—
my paintings placed in rows
across the dark smooth boards,
a quilt of squares and rectangles
alive with wonder.

I want others to wind around my art
as if they are walking a hidden trail—
discovering yellow anise and silvery spider webs
painted on grassy bamboo,
delicate poppy petals
transformed into monarch wings,
charcoal hills stained with blackberry juice,
wild mustard flowers splattered like stars
across a canvas of lupine sky.

In the twilight of my dream,
I watch the paintings flow together,
become a river of all that breathes and blossoms
in the soft dark earth.

The Lost Child

She is a lost child,
a fluttering sylph who once lived
among the water lilies.
Long ago, at the whim of a water god,
her wandering spirit was changed
into a bronze statue—
her face, her body, her long dress
carry the patina of another world,
colors of an ancient sea.

She is the little girl who stood in the garden
among my mother's purple pansies—
the silent playmate
who was my age, my height,
the one who spoke to me
without moving her lips,
who ran without ever taking a step
across the dark grassy lawn
in the Illinois summer twilight.
We chased fireflies and fairies,
the sky above us a lantern of stars.

Almost seventy years later
she is still a child,
though now she stands in *my* garden.
She is me and I am her—
the silent one who listens
to the trees speak,
who watches the leaves
blossom into a fiery sunset.

She is the little girl
who has always been left outside,
exposed to air and rain.
Her hollow eyes are filled
with a strange light,
her arms hold a trailing bouquet
of small delicate flowers that never die.
She remembers what I have forgotten,
those other sad autumns.

 I talk to her, touch her bronze lips
with my fingers—
notice the tiny red maple leaf
that's settled on her arm.

Ode to the Veiled Goddess

Oh, veiled goddess,
whose face is hidden,
whose name is nameless—

Your body is windswept,
fluid as water.
Incoming tides wrap around
your breasts and belly,
currents of desire
swirl up your thighs.

You raise your curved arms
above your head,
slowly sway your hips,
dance the mystery of ancient oceans—
and every woman who looks at you
eventually sees herself.

Moon Dance

Tonight, the moon
is throwing a party,
her invitation written on
a fiery sky streaked with blue—
the sun disappearing gracefully,
as an old lover might do—
the horizon the color of
a crimson balloon.

The streetlights are wrapped
in sapphire stars.
Hidden in the shadows,
a snowy egret whispers,
She will be fashionably late
in order to make a grand entrance!

Out on the water,
a tugboat passes by,
lights twinkling on its bow,
or is it a pleasure boat,
red lanterns swaying in the night breeze?

Laughter flows like wine
from the bars—
children stay out late
and play hide and seek in the trees,
waiting for the moon to find them.

At last she rises in the east,
her face round and gold,
a woman bold with desire.
She smiles on the town—
enamored with its colored lights
and loud singing.
All night long,
the old men try to dance with her,
drunk on silver memories.

Scorpio Angel

She spins on the wind
in her gown of silver clouds,
long strands of spider silk
dripping down her breasts.

Her body the soft blur
of a rain-soaked garden, seen through
the gauzy curtain of a dream,
her hair and eyes
the color of a starless night.

A crimson tree
is painted on her belly,
its wet leaves scattered down her thighs.

She disappears with the rain,
leaving a gift for me to find—
a basket filled with pomegranates,
ruby-red and ripe in the morning sun.

How they glisten like her lips.

Remembering Kyoto

Dancing kimono—
silky robe of desire
a lover wears.

Plum blossoms caught in its folds,
cascading waterfall of stars.

Cherry blossoms
sprinkled along the hem.

The sleeves,
delicate butterfly wings—
dreams from a thousand lifetimes
painted on each one.

Sailing to Akumal

We've built a boat that floats on air.
It needs no water, no anchor,
only billowing clouds for sails.

Let us go then, you and I,
to watch the slipping sun
be swallowed up
by the horizon.

The sunset spreads out before us
a grand feast—
bowls of sweet oranges and amber pears
placed in an indigo sky,
as darkness wraps us
in her satin cape,
appliquéd with stars.

We'll find Polaris,
sail south
to a Yucatan beach
where sea turtles
bury their eggs—

our boat an iridescent shell,
shining in the moonlight.

Tossing the Sticks

Rising up from brackish water,
the blustery wind
is an old crone
who tosses fortune sticks
on the ground.

She crouches over
sunbaked dirt—
lets broken marsh reeds
fall from her twisted fingers,
twirls and sings her incantations
in gusty breaths.

Five smooth sticks of different sizes
tossed on the ground like an open fan—
delicate paper blown to dust,
calligraphy and lotus blossoms gone.

What divinations can be read
by the way they land,
or which direction they point?
Which side tells the future—

side turned up to sky and sun,
or side touching earth?

These sticks
weren't tossed for me,
but here they are.
What question
should I ask the wind,
who tossed these sticks
for the world?

Acknowledgements

With gratitude to Mary Eichbauer, Deborah Schmidt, Laurie Hailey, Nina Serrano, and Deborah Fruchey, for helping to bring this book to fruition.

"Morning Walk in Lithia Park" received an Honorable Mention in the Journeys category, Ina Coolbrith Awards Banquet, 2021

"The Calligraphy of Winter" was a First Prize winner in the Nature category, Ina Coolbrith Awards Banquet, 2022

"What the Bee Discovers" received an Honorable Mention in the Discovery category, Ina Coolbrith Poets' Dinner, 2022

"California in Early May" received an Honorable Mention in the California category, Ina Coolbrith Awards Banquet, 2022

"Dancing with the Trees" first appeared in *The Poeming Pigeon, Issue 12,* 2022

"The Shell" received an Honorable Mention in the Nature category, Ina Coolbrith Awards Banquet, 2021

"A Sky the Color of Oceans" was first published in the column, *Going the Distance,* Benicia Herald, 2021

"A Flock of Magpies" received an Honorable Mention, Benicia Love Poetry Contest, 2021

"A Poet Revises Luncheon on the Grass" received an Honorable Mention in the Love category, Ina Coolbrith Poets' Dinner 2020

"Waiting for my Muse" was a First Prize winner in the People category, Ina Coolbrith Awards Banquet, 2021

"Field Guides" was a First Prize winner in the Love category, Ina Coolbrith Awards Banquet, 2022

"Whale-of-a-Heart" was a First Prize winner in the Love category, Ina Coolbrith Poets' Dinner, 2022

"Light, Hope, and Love" was first published in the Benicia Herald, and then in *Yearning to Breathe Free, A Community Journal of 2020,* Benicia Literary Arts, 2022

"Time of Poetry" was a First Prize winner, Dancing Poetry Festival, Artists Embassy International, 2021

"Dreaming in the Time of the Pandemic" was the First Prize winner, Benicia Love Poetry Contest, 2022

About the Author

Johanna Ely is the author of three previous poetry books, *Transformation, Tides of the Heart–Poems for Benicia,* and *Postcards From a Dream (Blue Light Press 2020).* She is an award-winning poet, who has been published in literary journals and anthologies, including *California Quarterly* and *The Poeming Pigeon.* She has been nominated for a Pushcart Prize, and was the 2022 winner of the Benicia Love Poetry Contest. Johanna served as the sixth poet laureate of Benicia, California, and is a board member of the Ina Coolbrith Circle of Poets, one of the oldest poetry groups in California.

(photo by Sam Morse)

Other Books by this Author

Chapbooks

Transformation
(Blurb, 2015)

Tides of the Heart—Poems for Benicia
(Blurb, 2019)

Books

Postcards from a Dream
(Blue Light Press, 2020)

What Still Matters
(Last Laugh Productions, 2023)

Editor

Light and Shadow
(Benicia Literary Arts, 2018)

Anthologies

A Word for All Seasons
(Benicia Literary Arts, 2014)

Crossing the Strait
(Benicia Literary Arts, 2016)

The Gathering—Ina Coolbrith Circle Anthology
Volumes: 14, 15
(Sheridan Press, 2017, 2022)

Light and Shadow
(Benicia Literary Arts, 2018)

California Fire & Water:
A Climate Crisis Anthology
(Story Street Press, 2020)

Pandemic Puzzle Poems
(Blue Light Press, 2021)

Yearning to Breathe Free:
A Community Journal of 2020
(Benicia Literary Arts, 2022)

Nooks & Crannies
(Benicia Literary Arts, 2023)

Other Offerings from Last Laugh Productions

We'll Always Have Stockton, by Steve Arntson

The Worlds According to Loki, 2nd Edition, by Vampyre Mike Kassel

For Whoever Thinks a Piano is Furniture, by Rudy Jon Tanner

The Hall of Painted Sonnets, Sonnets by Steve Arntson, Art by Diane Lee Moomey

Embodied, by Jan Dederick

Gypsy & Other Poems, by Steve Arntson

Armageddon Bootcamp…and other poems (hardcover, by Maria Elizabeth Rosales

Three Kinds of Dark (ebook, hardcover), by Deborah L. Fruchey

Touchstones (hardcover), by Maria Elizabeth Rosales

Priestess of Secrets, by Deborah L. Fruchey

Bat Flower: poems, plays & other perversions, by Vampyre Mike Kassel

Armadillo (ebook, hardcover), by Deborah L. Fruchey

Color Cards & Self Healing, by Jean Luo

The Colors of Sound (companion CD or MP3), performed & composed by Robert Hamaker

A Scandalous Creature, by Deborah L. Fruchey

Mental Illness Ain't for Sissies, by Deborah L. Fruchey

The Unwilling Heiress (paperback), by Deborah L. Fruchey

Island Journey (Instrumental CD or MP3), composed & performed by Robert M. Hamaker

Island Journey (Narrated Meditation CD or MP3), by Robert M. Hamaker & Deborah Fruchey

Crystal Connections (CD or MP3), by Robert M. Hamaker & Erik Satie *(gymnopodie #1)*

Crystalline Sleep (Binaural Beats CD or MP3), by Robert M. Hamaker

Opus De Funk (CD or MP3), composed by Horace Silver, performed by
Interplay

www.lastlaughproductions.org

www.ingramcontent.com/pod-product-compliance
Lightning Source LLC
Chambersburg PA
CBHW052123090426
42741CB00009B/1928